Gilda Lyons

b.1975

Songs from the F Train

on Poems by Children from Brooklyn
for Voice and Piano

ED30039

ISMN 979-0-060001-063-9

www.schott-music.com

Mainz · London · Madrid · New York · Paris · Prague · Tokyo · Toronto
© 2010 SCHOTT MUSIC CORPORATION, New York · Printed in USA

Foreword

The idea for American Opera Projects (AOP), Fort Greene Park Conservancy and The Walt Whitman Project to commission Gilda Lyons came from previous happy associations with the composer. Gilda had spent a year in AOP's "Composer and the Voice" program housed in our Fort Greene, Brooklyn home base. We admired Gilda's strengths as an emerging song writer: clear, natural text setting and lyric instincts that caught the emotion of words in surprising ways. The thing that most drew us to Gilda for this project was her affinity for simple stories, especially ones that have a black mood or sad central theme, but are brightened by the narrator's clear-eyed story telling or by an ending highlighting the silver lining of a dark cloud. The young poets, Alexis Cummings, Samori Covington and Najaya Royal, came to the attention of Greg Trupiano, Director of The Walt Whitman Project and a frequent partner for AOP events in the Fort Greene area. Greg had connected with Angeli Rasbury, a poet and mentor of young writers. Angeli's students were invited to read their poetry aloud in Fort Greene Park in the summer of 2008. These were exciting poetry readings: the girls were sending important messages about life even though they were not yet teenagers. The poems were universal. It took only a few days after hearing for us to be convinced to commission musical settings. Gilda Lyons accepted our commission taking the three poems that make up the cycle, "Songs of the F Train" and transforming them into an anthem, a defiant battle cry, and a valentine – expressions of the Brooklyn spirit. Brooklyn is a borough where people are proud, dangerous yet vulnerable and playfully passionate.

A performance note: performers of this song cycle should allow themselves to be stirred to the core by the texts...be fierce and take risks with your music making. This action brings you closer to the state of mind of the poets and the creative channels through which a gifted composer makes it possible for us to share common life experiences through music.

Charles Jarden
General Director, American Opera Projects
www.operaprojects.org
Brooklyn, 2010

TEXTS

1. I'm Smart

I'm smart but timid,
I worry I will never break
out of my fear.

I hear the
harmony when
people sing.

I see the
violence in my
community.

I want to indulge
my talents to the
world, I'm smart
but timid.

- Alexis Cummings, age 12

2. I am From The Ghetto "Brooklyn"

I am from the streets of Brooklyn.
Where Graffiti Art is our museum.
Where that park on the corner with
broken bottles and needles from
the crack heads is our Disney World.
Where gang fights are our get together,
and funerals are our family reunions.
I am from the streets of Brooklyn
where we use jumper cables to play
double dutch because, jump ropes keep
the crooks near so they could sell it for crack.
I am from the streets of Brooklyn
where the ghetto is something
I can runaway from
though can not forget.

- Najaya Royal, age 12

3. When Randa wears red

When Randa wears red
She looks like a strawberry
When Randa wears red
She looks beautiful
When Randa wears red
She is happy
When Randa wears red
She gets new things
When Randa wears red
She remembers everything
When Randa wears red
She has her watch
When Randa wears red
She reads a book
When Randa wears red
She matches with Valentines Day

- Samori Covington, age 9

Commissioned by American Opera Projects,
Fort Greene Park Conservancy and The Walt Whitman Project.

Songs from the F Train

on poems by children from Brooklyn

1. I'm Smart

Alexis Cummings, age 12

Gilda Lyons (2009)

want, I see, I hear, I wor-ry, I sing.

I want to in-dulge my tal-ents to the world,

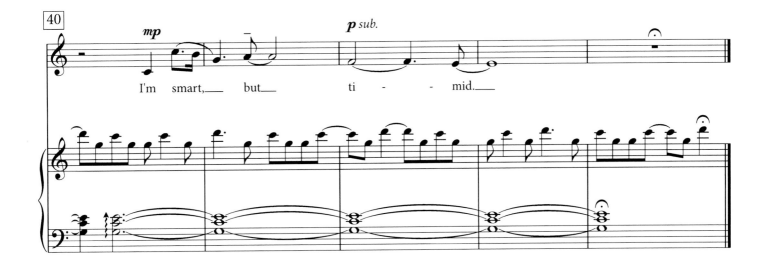

I'm smart, but ti - - mid.

2. I am From the Ghetto "Brooklyn"

Najaya Royal, age 12

Gilda Lyons (2009)

gang fights_ are our get to-geth-er and fu-ner-als_ are our fam-i-ly___ re - un - ions.

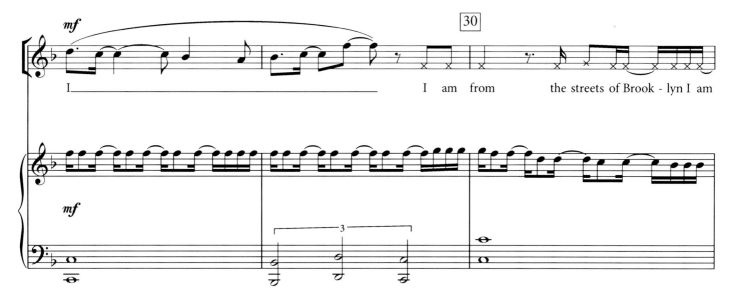

I am from the streets of Brook - lyn I am

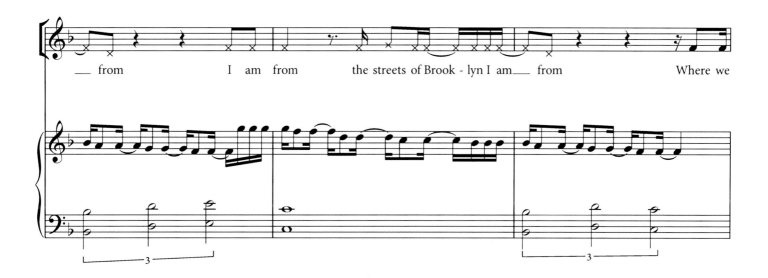

from I am from the streets of Brook - lyn I am from Where we

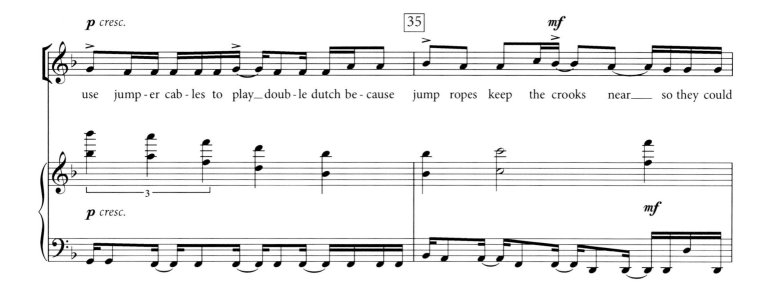

use jump - er cab - les to play double dutch be - cause jump ropes keep the crooks near so they could

sell it for crack. I am____ from the streets of__ Brook - lyn

40

I_____ I am____ from the

streets of__ Brook - lyn I____ I_____ I_____

ossia:

I_____

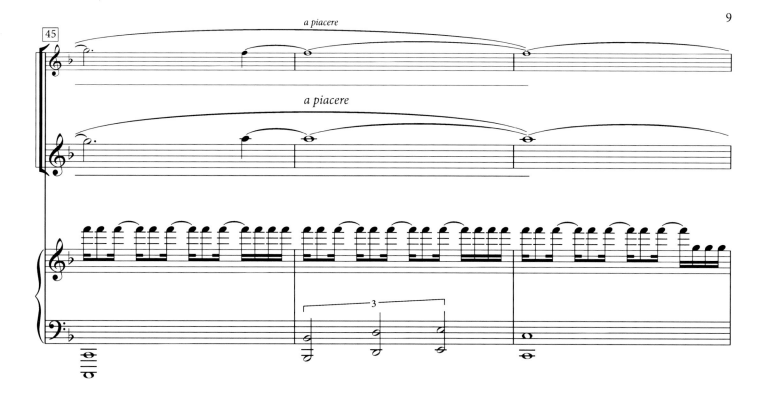

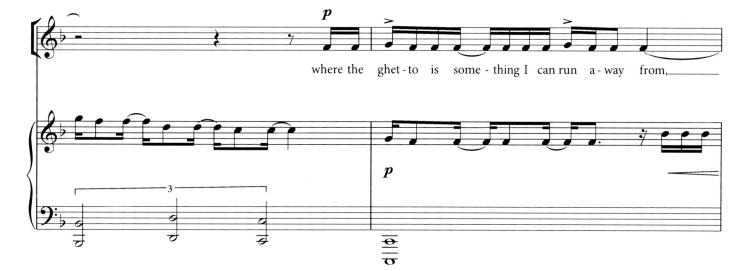

where the ghet-to is some-thing I can run a-way from,

where the ghet-to is some-thing I can run a-way from,

3. When Randa wears red

Samori Covington, age 9

Gilda Lyons (2009)

*) Pronounced "Rhonda"

hap - py._____ When Ran-da wears red, When Ran-da wears red, When Ran - da wears

red_____ When Ran-da wears red_____ She_____

gets_____ new things When Ran-da wears red She_ re - mem - - bers

e - very thing_____ When_____ she

wears   new   things,   When Ran - da wears red, When Ran - da wears

red,   When Ran - da wears___ red   She_____ has her

Val - en-tine's Day   When Ran - da wears red   She match-es with   Val - en-tine's

Day   When Ran - da wears_____ red

Gilda Lyons (b. 1975), composer, vocalist, and visual artist, combines elements of renaissance, neo-baroque, spectral, folk, agitprop Music Theater, and extended vocalism to create works of uncompromising emotional honesty and melodic beauty. Tom Strini of the *Milwaukee Journal Sentinel* describes her "Nahuatl Hymn to the All-Mother" for treble choir (Clarion CLCD-936), commissioned by The Milwaukee Choral Artists, as "hair-raising, yet elegant [with] slides, dips, yips and yelps amid ceremonial intensity."

Ms. Lyons has received commissions from American Opera Projects, The ASCAP Foundation / Charles Kingsford Fund, Amy Pivar Dances, ComposersCollaborative Inc., Finisterra Piano Trio, Fort Greene Park Conservancy, The Seasons Music Festival, Paul Sperry, Sweet Plantain String Quartet, Two Sides Sounding, and The Walt Whitman Project, among others. Composer-in-Residencies include the Seasons Music Festival in Washington State and the Hartford Women Composers Festival.

An active vocalist and fierce advocate of contemporary music, Ms. Lyons has commissioned, premiered, and workshopped new vocal works by dozens of composers. Of her recent performance in Daron Hagen's "Shining Brow" (Buffalo Philharmonic/Falletta) (Naxos) David Shengold of *Opera, UK* writes "Gilda Lyons's clear soprano compels admiration."

While best known for her work as composer and performer, Gilda Lyons also serves as Artistic and Executive Director of The Phoenix Concerts on Manhattan's Upper West Side and as Executive Director of The Lotte Lehmann Foundation.

Ms. Lyons made her professional debut as composer and vocalist with the American Symphony Chamber Orchestra in 1997, performing the world premiere of her orchestral song cycle "Feis." She received her Ph.D. in Music Composition from the State University of New York at Stony Brook and is a graduate of the University of Pittsburgh and Bard College. *www.gildalyons.com*